Borderline Personality Disorder

The Texts And Emails

This book is an account of my experiences dating someone with borderline personality disorder. More specifically as the title says it is composed of the text messages and emails that I received for the last six months of our relationship. You can see the disorder very clearly in these messages and I will describe, or clarify, some of the situations that the messages had pertained to. This book is in no way meant to offend anybody, it is to show the roller coaster of emotions, the delusional thoughts and the hardships of being involved with a person who does not treat their borderline personality disorder, and also how it affects the person dating a person with untreated b.p.d. This information should not be used to treat, diagnose, or define Borderline Personality Disorder in any way since I am not a medical, psychological or psychiatric doctor.

Now I feel that it's appropriate to give a little info about the relationship and our history together. As to protect the identity of this woman, I will refer to her as Kay. I have also changed the names of everybody else in the texts, accept for my own. I am going to keep the relationship summary pretty short and to the point, again, as to focus on the texts and emails.

I dated Kay for about three and a half years. The relationship was good at first but soon declined into an emotionally, physically, and verbally abusive relationship. In the three and a half years of dating Kay, we broke up at least a dozen times. I can't even remember how many times we argued or how many times Kay beat me up. Kay was seeking treatment for her b.p.d. when we first met but for the most part of our relationship she did not. Kay suffered from bouts of depression and constantly used drugs and alcohol to self-medicate. Kay was also "boy crazy", as she liked to call it, for about the last year. This relationship was toxic and we defiantly worked our way into a bad dynamic. The texts and emails in this book were from near the end of our relationship. After these texts and emails we saw each other for about three days, following my return from an out of state job, but Kay was physically abusive and we had to stop seeing each other entirely.

So now that you know a little bit about the relationship I will share some texts and emails with you. Keep in mind that for the sake of this book I left a lot of stuff out of the relationship summary, since I want this to be more about the text and emails. If a text or email needs some clarifying I will add a note but for the most part I'd just like to share the experience. This is about six months of texts and emails. This was a very difficult six months for me and Kay, as well. The texts start off randomly and go on until we blocked one another's emails. Here are my last texts and emails from my relationship with b.p.d.

Note: My responses will say "Me:" by the date and messages from Kay just have the date.

4/28/11

i miss you, too, though. Why did you have to make me hate you? We had good chemistry that I don't have with other guys. They like me but I don't like them. You just said and did SO much fucked up stuff, and the craigslist shit is just outrageously creepy and pathetic.

4/30/11

Where are you?

I know you have been trying to meet people on craigslist, you freak. You just want me because you are starting to realize that craigslist isn't gonna work for you, or that your weiner isn't very big or hard without a lot of special attention that another girl probably isn't gonna give you.

I am sick of you and never want to see you again.

I hate you.

Fuck you.

Note: Kay always had delusions that I was finding girls on craigslist for sexual meetings. I have actually never met anybody from craigslist besides to sell them a car.

4/30/11

btw, only crazy people and ugly people use craigslist. Either that, or ugly whores who are trying to add more loser guys to their harem. Good luck with YOUR STUPID LIFE! You really did have a good thing with me and boy were you a fucking retard. I am so glad I am out of that horrible relationship and back in the real world

4/30/11

Ok. I will be nice because I know I have your baby here and I should be civil. I am just so mad that you are talking to me again after the extortion and other psycho shit you said. I am just burning with rage. I think it's best that you do NOT talk to me and use social workers to communicate. Not only do I hate you with a passion, but I totally think you are a freak.

Seriously. The chick you met on craigslist is uuuuuugly and you have gone TOO far. YOu moved in with those two crazy guys and turned into a totally unredeemable freak. I thought you were ok when you were in EP but you did nothing but creep online and be a psycho since you left. I even went to D-town for 5 days and hit up Tower and have a GREAT time and fucking everyone was there to tell me I was awesome and I loved it. Even Matt showed up and told me I was hot out of nowhere. It was eye opening for sure! The minute I'm seen in Soup without you EVERYONE comes out to tell me that I was way better than you and "totally righteous" and that they had "nothing bad to say about me". Even Lee at the palace told me I was awesome and that he was sorry for being a prick and that you were creepy.

I'm pissed. Give me a few more days maybe

4/30/11 *Me:*

dont burn with rage kay.

i havent met anybody on craigslist. what are you talking about?

i stayed on their couch for two weeks while i found a job kay. i didnt really have much of a choice. deric was ALWAYS either at work or boning fat chicks somewhere, and allen stopped smoking pot and drinking, started working out all the time and he takes pills so hes not really even that crazy anymore. i am not an unredeemable freak though. i am doing all the things a responsible adult should be doing. i have a job. in like a couple weeks ill have a place. i was offered a supervisor job in a shop in ****** that i turned down so that i could be close to my daughter and mav, and you if you ever want me to be.

what do you mean i was ok when i was in ep but i did nothing but creep online and be a psycho since i left? i havent been online besides checking my email and looking for jobs.

yeah thats what people do. they wait until a girl is single and tell her all the nicest things in the world. theyre not lying you are hot and awesome and all that jazz but come on now kay, thats what guys do. like you didnt know that all those guys wanted to fuck you before we broke up. and in all reality they are soup people. thats what they do. they go to work all week so that when the weekend comes they can go out to the bar and see the same people and if someone new shows up or if someone comes back for 5 days or whatever then they want to tell them that theyre hot or awesome or whatever. and thats their life. but im the loser right?

okay, lee from the palace is creepy. just look at him. i wasnt creepy i hated going out. especially to that lame ass bar. i loved hanging out with you and drinking but it was so stressful but in all reality fuck soup. its a skuzzy nasty town full of losers. and you knew that at one point. of course people are going to be nice to you and shower you with compliments while youre there because you are awesome but they still are shit.

so did you hook up with anybody in soup?

also tim is in ep with you isnt he?

alright if you need a few days then theyre yours. i just wish i could go back and fix all of this. i hate hearing you say things that make me feel like shit. i miss you and just want things to be the way they were.

5/1/11

I didn't actually stay in Soup for long. We were there for less than two hours and it was like suddenly I was a rock star. We went back to D-town at midnight. I know Soup is shitty. It was ridiculous. I felt like I was in the twilight zone. You said you "went out' and met somebody so I pictured you hanging out with Randy and your retard friend from the circus and thought I would make you feel like a relative failure at Tower ave, since you used to be one of the Superior drunken rabble.

Do you think you'd be able to get your daughter to drink milk?

5/2/11

I feel sick so I am not going to the Bou's house tonight. If you want to help with Belle tonight that will be fine. You could stop by after 7, but if you think you are even the slightest bit capable of going insane with anger again then don't come.

5/2/11

I miss you. I hope you make it here between 7 and 8

5/2/11

Okay. I guess you were just bullshitting about seeing your baby tonight. Screw you, then. I'm really not surprised. I wasn't expecting you to come through.

5/3/11

How do we see each other again?

5/3/11 *Me:*
i just got your messages. i will get on my way over. im way too tired to go insane.

5/3/11

I wanna see you again but what is your plan? I have a little bit of money.... Not much though.

5/3/11

I'm going to pick up the kids now but if you think of something let me know. It's a nice day so all I need is for you to pull up the pdq.... Maybe knock on my window or tape a little note to it if you are around.... idk.

5/3/11

My dad and mav are going to a movie soon. Could you be here when they leave? You can sleep in my room again and I'll feed you

5/3/11

They left already. Please come over. I need to see you again

5/3/11

It's been over an hour since you said "A bit" so I hope that means you will be here soon!

5/6/11

Come home?

5/9/11

I'm sure you can just sneak into my room

5/9/11

Today was great! I studied with Lindsey and then met with my soon-to-be summer math tutor. Then I ran about 2 miles down grand avenue, and then 2 miles back. Let's go drink there next time! Maybe we will meet a Tibetian monk from Macallister who will buy our drinks! After that went to philosophy and then ran 6 more miles with no shoes!! I have major blisters but I feel awesome. Then I picked up the kids. Did you know that Molly can shake her head "No"? She does it intelligently. Totally on purpose. She is soooooooo smart. We are watching over the hedge.

Molly's milk at daycare expired. Do you think you could get a half gallon on your way home? If not I can go out and get some, but it will be easier. My dad isn't here and the kids have to go to bed soon. It has to be a half gallon. The big ones are too big for their mini fridge.

How are you?

5/10/11

I love you so much. Did you know that?

Golf ball sized hail out here

5/10/11

I was just thinking that. I was wondering how I would know with no tv or radio. I figured you would just show up and save us. I love you.

Did you tell them you want to quit your job?

5/11/11

Ohh, that's terrible! You must be having a heart attack. You have to admit, that temp agency was a good idea. They really hook up those jobs. I can't wait for you to get home and get in bed. It is so amazing to sneak-live with you. It makes me want to real live with you again. Those were good days. Be careful, ok?

5/11/11

I am sorry for dumping everything on you this morning. I really am. I just wanted to get to the school so I could do my final and I really appreciate you helping me out this week! I know I have been irresponsible and all that bizniz but I get crazy at finals. I have a final tomorrow and a Spanish final next tuesday. I will make it up to you soon, though, ok?

How did it all go?

5/11/11

He drives me totally bananas in the morning. I get so pissed that I lose my cool sometimes. It isn't good.

My test went just fine. Thank god we practiced. I have a lot of stress over registration right now, though. ughhh.

5/11/11

My dad is out still so be careful. Try not to cross paths with him or anything. Going to bed now

5/25/11

I miss you too

5/31/11

God damn, I fucking miss you too

5/31/11

Reality is that you repeated Tucson and proved to me that love isnt enough when the guy is shit

6/1/11

It hurts everywhere. What the fuck? You just get your family back and you mercilessly beat the mother of your kids AGAIN? YOu must

6/1/11

be insane

NOTE: what she is talking about here is from a night were we just made up from a fight and we went to a nice hotel for a day, we ended up getting drunk and wanted to go swimming but Kay wanted me to put the clothes from the washer into the dryer, and then check on the kids. I completed these two tasks very fast and had half of a cigarette out on the balcony of the room. When I met Kay down at the pool she was irate. She insisted that I was gone for a half an hour, and that I was probably drinking with women in the bar, when in reality it was ten minutes and I was completing tasks that she requested of me. We went back up to the hotel room and her anger got worse. She started hitting me and I got away from her, she got up and was hitting me and I grabbed her computer and threatened to smash it if she continued to hit me. She then grabbed the arm that I had the computer held over my head with and sunk her teeth into it. Ive never felt pain like that before. She didn't let go of my arm so I grabbed the back of her neck and squeezed, she then let go. I was about to call her crazy when she bit my other arm and I face pushed her off of me, I smashed the computer on the floor, and left the room. I was going to go sleep in my car but my keys and money and stuff were still in the room so i turned around to go back to the room and security was waiting for me. I told him I just needed my stuff but he said he didn't care and I had to leave. I let him escort me out and while on the elevator the security guard called me a piece of shit. I said u don't know shit and your just a security guard so shut the fuck up. Then he punched me and slammed my head against the wall, he tried to put me in a choke hold and that's when I started pushing him off of me. We got down to the ground level and his co-worker got to join in on beating me up then they cuffed me and kicked me some more. My eyebrow was split open and when the cops got there my relief was only momentary since when I said, "thank God, the cops are here, these guys just beat the shit out of me." The police officer stepped on my mouth and told me to shut up. I was arrested and the first cop's partner had a moment of honesty and decency when she raised the question, "so who beat the shit out of him?" the look of concern and confusion on her face gave me a short lived faith in the judicial system which was gone as quick as it came when her partner said, "who cares?" without even thinking. I went to jail overnight and then in the morning I was released because all charges against me were dropped by the district attorney. But Kay still remembers what she remembers, regardless of what actually happens she can never be wrong and she can never be at fault within her mind.

6/1/11

What am I gonna do??

6/1/11

What about me?

6/1/11

Help me somebody please

6/1/11

Stop hurting us you dumb mother fucker

6/1/11

You are chaos.

6/1/11

But you have to pick up the kids

6/1/11

I just quit

6/2/11

Mav was freezing cold and wet

6/2/11

Thats okay. I held him all night.

6/3/11

Could you pick up the kids today? I have to stay a little late at anytime

6/3/11

Thank you. Maybe you could bring them food too?

6/3/11

Garage sales with amy. Not much. I decided I want to move to Highland Park in St Paul

6/3/11

Or near the como zoo? Does the como zoo have a daycare?

6/3/11

How did it go babo?

6/3/11

That makes me happy!

6/3/11

You are perfect for that gym

6/3/11

He can mix it up. Thats something trainers know how to do

6/3/11

Idk yet. The time he wanted me to do wont work... I was gonna tell him tomorrow

6/3/11

Im pretty bummed about that too.

6/3/11

Maybe if I move to St Paul and get a new daycare

6/3/11

Where you at?

6/3/11

Why did you go there?

6/3/11

Im at amys house

6/3/11

Buy my laptop please?

6/3/11

Tomorrow, please? I need it for Math.

NOTE: I did replace the computer.

6/4/11

Still up?

 6/4/11

Hi! Whats up?

6/4/11

Hello?

6/4/11

Isnt it? I like to be sore every day. Yes I do want to go to st paul with you. Where can we meet?

6/4/11

Im at the zoo working my way to the door

6/4/11

Dont know

6/4/11

Dont say my name

6/4/11

You are a fucking idiot

6/4/11

I haaaate you

6/4/11

Look, fuckstick. I could use some help so meet me here now.

6/4/11

Meet me at the st thomas gas station at 4 and dont be late

6/4/11

Im driving you asshole

6/4/11

Where u at?

6/6/11

Hey, I can't find my phone and I know it is somewhere in my car. Could you call it a few times at 2pm, please please???

6/7/11

Goodnight!

6/7/11

Eye of the tiger baybee

6/7/11

Me too. I can barely believe my memory

6/7/11

Whats wrong??

 6/8/11

I definitely need a deep dicking

6/8/11

Its okay! going okay

6/8/11

Driving a lot

6/8/11

Woah! How could we do it?

6/8/11

I like that!!

6/8/11

I like that a lot

6/8/11

The Y idea works

6/8/11

Ok ymca sex it is

NOTE: we didn't.

6/8/11

Im smiling like a dumbass now haha

6/8/11

:)

6/8/11

I love you baby. I cant wait for it

6/9/11

Where are you?

6/9/11

Amy is still up

6/9/11

She just went in her room but is still up

6/9/11

Havent tried yet. Will you always love me plz?

6/9/11

Of course. You are the one baby.

 6/9/11

The car just died again

6/9/11

When do you get off work?

6/9/11

Nooooo wait 20 minutes please bebe

6/10/11

How??? omg I think you just ruined my life......

6/10/11

Dammit I need to sleep and now Im crying and panicking

6/10/11

Why would you overdraw when it is in both of our names????

NOTE: She got a couple thousand dollars from her mom, and I was checking my balance in my account when I notice that there was $1500 when it should have been -$500 because I had just taken out a payday advance, I simply told Kay that she should transfer the money to another account otherwise they would take that advance out of the balance. And the account wasn't both of ours, it was mine and she was only on there because when I set up the account the banker asked if I wanted her to have access to the account and I said sure. The reason she put that money into my account was because he had overdraft fees on her other account so she thought she could avoid her bills by using my account.

6/10/11

Did I leave my laptop in your car?

6/10/11

You owe me 150 now

6/10/11

Thanks for being a dick today

6/15/11

I know. I'm still hurting today, too. It never gets any less painful

6/15/11

Im trying. These times are hard. Duluth will be fun though

6/15/11

No. Im going to turn in my resume at the ywca. If you find a bike and trailer on craigslist we could all go together

6/15/11

I know. Next week

6/15/11

Dropping off one more app then going to work

6/15/11

Just stop! isnt it obvious that You arent my type? you make me crazy

6/15/11

Why dont you go read playboys in a gas station until they kick you out you asshole

6/15/11

Because you like porn!!

6/15/11

I remembered chris telling me about you trying to steal porn and it made it harder to tolerate you

NOTE: my brother jokingly told her that we stole playboys from a gas station when we were kids.

6/15/11

You called me a dickhead

6/15/11

Remember when I told you that you had to give it up or I would never forget it? I told you this! And I said to never ever let me find out out if you do it! I was so good to you and now I am sooooo crazy and jealous and hate you. It got progressively worse until it was the most demented freakshow it could be and you didnt even fuck me. You even physically pummelled me in a room with the kids two times and tonight you think you can call me a dickhead. Really? you are such a white trash superior no respect ahole

NOTE: She is talking about me looking at porn two years prior to this message. And the pummelling that she is referring to is the hotel where I got bit by her and beat by security, and while we were in Tuscon words were exchanged, she jumped on me and choked me, I pushed her off, then she jumped on me and clawed her face, then when I pushed her off she fell. Hardly a pummeling, but not from the way she tells it.

6/15/11

I am not getting over it even a little bit

6/15/11

And I dont want to date a smoker

6/17/11

Hey, i love you

6/18/11

Sorry for being terrible. I feel better after seeing Tyler for 2 minutes.

6/18/11

My grandma is batty

6/18/11

Makes whatever gripe with you seem trivial. Sorry for abusing you like that pretty guy

6/18/11

Also I had one beer and feel all better

6/18/11

We have to get out together

6/18/11

Thanks. I have so much energy. I need to run far. I cant sleep! what arE you doing and why arent you pretty?

6/18/11

Ahh the flower. Im no longer pretty.

6/18/11

Omg I want to run punch too! I had two beers and keep doing sumo pushups and burpees and I cant get tired but I need this energy tomorrow

6/18/11

Cant sleep ahhhh

6/18/11

Hey. whats up?

6/18/11

Today

6/18/11

Why cant you be nice?

6/18/11

Im coming in a bit

6/21/11

i hatethat youtookmy last canofpop. That was low

NOTE: I've noticed that her texts and emails lack spacing between the words when she is so mad that she goes into seizures. Doctors say that it's epilepsy but I don't know how accurate that is.

6/21/11

Not the greatest.

6/21/11

We will be okay. Im filling out an app. Thanks for being nice. It helps

6/21/11

stpaul

6/21/11

that is wednesday baby

6/21/11

i work in chaska today

6/21/11

I have to pick up the kids

6/21/11

Right

6/21/11

Loveyou

6/21/11

home

6/21/11

You dont respect me and you pretend you will if I take you back. Look whatyou did to my life.

6/21/11

Just stay away and the drama will end. I know you think I will love you even though you treat me like some shitty bar slut. Just stop

6/21/11

You were yelling in my face!

6/21/11

you never stop treating me like shit! You talk to me just like my dad and tyler. If I annoy you so bad then stay away

NOTE: she Is referring to disagreeing with her. She would tell me, her dad and her brother all of the things that were wrong with us and if we didn't praise her for her thoughts then we were all being mean and such.

6/21/11

you think talking like a slackjaw yokel is not wrong and I have different rules

6/21/11

stopcalling me kay and yeah,you sounded real concerned

6/21/11

you hurt me every time you talk like that to me but you have no idea what respect sounds like bc you were raised so mean

6/22/11

well nobody has ever talked to me as shitty as you do and it is sad that you never learned that. That is why ppl say you are an ass

6/22/11

ok then. You were raised by juve. Still dont know how to treat a woman with respect

6/22/11

You never listen. I want respect. You do it in front of my friends so you know how to fake it

6/22/11

they call me cay but nobody ever called me kay

6/22/11

can you PLEASE explore more respectful speechpatterns?

6/22/11

yeah. It was weird, but that is what my family andfriends called me

6/22/11

ernie.

6/22/11

fine

6/22/11

that was an lol

6/22/11

bernie mac

6/22/11

yes you can sleep with us

6/22/11

me and bernie mac

6/22/11

You sent that to the wrong person you freak!

6/22/11

It is raining

6/22/11

lookingfor jobs

6/22/11

im driving from place to place. I do not. Dont say that.

6/22/11

All over st paul

6/22/11

thank you. I found a good daycare

6/22/11

tim d. rescheduled

6/22/11

chaska

6/22/11

Just filling out apps

6/23/11

Yeah. Im definitely not screwing anybody else. I just wasnt ready yet for you to start stabbing me with your dick

6/23/11

hey,no come near me again, ok?

6/23/11

ihateyou and I will get you back 10 times for this you weaselpiece of shit

6/23/11

ruins my day when you cheat

NOTE: so what she's talking about here is that a telemarketer called her because I used her phone number for a while, the telemarketer apparently doesn't like her job and had some fun messing with Kay about stuff, the telemarketer asked to speak with me and apparently Kay asked her if I met her (the telemarketer) on craigslist, the girl said yeah and made a couple more wise cracks then hung up. I got this text right at the beginning of a shift and Kay ended up forwarding me the phone number after a few hours and I called it to see who my new girlfriend was but all I got was a reminder to pay my bills from a telemarketer, I convinced Kay to call the number afterward to prove that it was in fact a business and not a loose woman from craigslist. I never got an apology for any of the things she said.

6/23/11

echeating,like always. You know what you did. Just stop

6/23/11

You are just using me until you are cozy. Then little cheating can grow

6/23/11

liar

6/23/11

You think you covered your ass but you didn't

6/23/11

wow.

6/23/11

you are fucked up. Plz dont stalk us today

6/23/11

i have mace

NOTE: I bought her mace. Probably wasn't the best idea but I wanted her to have something for jogging at night. But I stood pretty firm on not buying her a gun!

6/23/11

GOD DAMMIT GOAWAY!

6/23/11

QUIT TRYING TO RUIN MY DAY! I HATE YOU!

6/23/11

Dontyou have work?

6/23/11

wow true colors

6/23/11

STOP! LEAVE ME ALONE

6/23/11

YOUGAVETHEBITCHMYNUMBER

6/23/11

PLZ STOP TALKING TO ME

6/23/11

WOW. EVIL

6/23/11

STUNNED

6/23/11

JUST PLEASE STOP

6/23/11

Ohpoor you

6/23/11

Okay then you should have no problem letting me be free!
Please do not harass me anymore. I was sad and now I
realize you are just crazy

6/23/11

youwillgetfiredifyoudontstopthis psychoshit

6/23/11

idofeelaweirdfeelingbehindmyeyes

6/23/11

tk took my ativanshot

6/23/11

ohno thisisbad

6/23/11

Iwillgotothedoc

6/23/11

i did. They will have ativanready for me at 6 bu then i cant
drive

6/23/11

icantakeitasapillifmylegs arent shakingyet

6/23/11

chaska. My jawistig htening too

6/23/11

i am coming

NOTE: this is where the telemarketer girlfriend hate texts stop.

6/24/11

molly just said doggy

6/24/11

wow. I just read that text that says "you are gonna lose me if you keep this crazy shit up" and you know what? I dont want you

NOTE: I sent the above text while she was accusing me of dating the telemarketer. Even though a well-balanced person may think, well they sent that to me while I was in a state of delusion, just prior to a seizure, and I was blindly accusing them of something that not only did they do but something that I would not tell them what I was accusing them of. Maybe it was a little crazy, and maybe behavior like this will lead me to a life of loneliness if it continues. Or something of this sort anyway.

6/24/11

you were psycho for six months and I still havent decided if I was gonna date you again. I know you will just screw up everything anyway

6/25/11

where are you?

7/1/11

Shuddup

7/1/11

you speak to me like a white trash ahole with no class speaks to his old lady and I will not tolerate it.

7/1/11

wow

7/1/11

too bad. I dont put up with this. Find a girl who wants to do it your way bc Im not going to do it.

7/1/11

I already made plans without you, jerk. Should have cherished me

7/4/11

shut up plz for fucking once in your life

7/5/11

Right. You can beat me up and say whatever you want and obviously try to make me think I deserve it (psycological abuse) me and still act like there is a "we" and I'm supposed to stop having a great time for a douchebag like you. I have had a super amazing weekend and it's all because I got some space!! WOOO!!! I totally never realized how much fun it would be to just go on dates with nice guys who like kids but wow!! We had mad fun and no risk of having to battle with the drunk and impossible!!! WOOOOO!!!!

7/5/11

I said I don't like you, bitch. You are delusional!

7/5/11

lol to the impulsive gratification quest and the drug friends. Just having summer fun with the kiddos. Good times and great people. Good thing you gave up your sobriety and got drunk and left me!

7/5/11 *Me:*

Okay that was a really hurtful message btw. Im not psychologically abusive and i love our kids. You seem to think that im responsible for the void in ur life but im not. If u made friends based on similar interests n common personality traits then u wouldnt feel like u had to b WOOOOed all the time by men. But instead ur friends revolve around drugs n alcohol. It really hurts that u did this to us. N it hurts more to c u try to blame me for your poor decisions. U intended on starting a fight so that u could have this awesome date weekend n in the process gave up a gym, moving out of the country, your major, n the smiles the kids get everyday when i walk thru the door. I wish u would think about what ur doing.

7/5/11

YOU ARE CRAZY FOR SAYING I STARTED THAT HAHAHA.

Just for that I am going to laugh as I read these allowed to everyone hahahahaha

7/5/11 *Me:*

Oh yeah real smart taking the kids on some first dates. Wow. Its just wrong from every angle.

7/5/11

I have known the guy my entire life! He used to live next door to my great grandma! He has a kid, too, and would never date a childless woman. It's all really nice and fun! We had a great time. There was no romancing, just kid stuff. Just having a nice day taking the kids around the cities without you.

Tell me I'm wrong and bad all you want but I am a pretty awesome girl. I'm a good mom and I'm pretty awesome all around. I'm gonna stop bothering with you now because in a fight with crazy you know crazy always wins. No point in talking to you.

7/5/11 *Me:*

Ur so 2 faced n it really sucks cuz i love one of them but the other makes life suck so bad. N u do the worst bad shit when ur mad as if its ok cuz ur mad.

7/5/11

YOU ARE SO THICK!! I'm not mad, silly billy. I hereby
dump you. Talk to me no more! I request formally that you
withdraw your annoyingness. Not just mad. WANT TO BE
DONE

7/5/11

LOLZIES!!! I'm awesome! You must be thinking of yourself!!
You are the one who is all that stuff, whatever it was. Didnt't
read it. It was typed too stupid.

7/5/11

sweet!! I guess I don't deserve you. Ahaahhahahahahah

7/5/11

You said earlier that you hate the kids and that you hope
Molly is not yours. You are too intense and off the wall right
now. Until you start talking like a real chill weekend dad you
will not get anything. Supervised social worker visits,
maybe, but you are nutters. Go take your van and find the
next willing woman! I do not care what you do with
anybody! Drink all you want and fuck anybody who wants
it. I do not care. I don't want you.

NOTE: I never in my life said that I hate my kids, I did
question whether or not my daughter is in fact my daughter
and I still do to this day.

42

7/6/11

You are a fucking idiot!!

YOU DID THIS! I DIDN'T DO ANYTHING!

Yeah, I started going out with other people but really that doesn't matter. The issue is your attitude, your lack of respect, your MOUTH, your temper, your DRINKING, etc. Why are you so jealous? Why is it so important that I don't call my friends when you rage on me? Why is it so important to you that I don't see other people? Seriously. Get a grip. Go find the next willing woman and stop trying to convince me that I am crazy and you are a victim. GO AWAY FROM ME!! YOU PROMISED THAT YOU WOULD!

You are an "okay" dad but you aren't that great. You are mean to Maven and don't listen when I try to interfere. That is why you started disrespecting me. I will defend Maven. I am not your mom who let your stepdad be a dick. All that shit about you calling me crazy is just you being a cruel mind-fucker. Go awayyyyyy!!! GO AWAY!!! You are ther worst thing in the world!!! You are so dangerous! You can't control yourself and I don't want to put us at risk anymore. I know when my kids are older and start defying you shit will hit the fan because you have to be the boss. Gabbi and Chris were telling me even before this fight that you had a scary hot temper and that I should get away before you blew up on me. They were right. There are a lot of guys who would be BETTER with the kids and wont fly off the handle and cross the line every two weeks.

GO AWAYYYYYYY

PLEASE!!! LEAVE US ALONE!!

43

7/6/11

You promised yesterday that you were leaving forever!!! Fucking do it already!!!

7/7/11

What do you want me to do for it?

7/7/11 *Me:*

I want to see the kids

7/7/11

I'm sorry. I don't want to.

7/7/11

I could get a little bit of money. I'd rather do that. Could you hook me up? I can't sleep well lately

7/7/11

No more than 20 bucks. Less would be better

7/7/11

ok then. 20

7/7/11

I don't have cash

7/9/11

Can you come back soon, please?

7/9/11

Can you please come soon? My phone died

7/22/11

I hope you hate yourself, too.

You poured a baby's milk down the drain.

I told you I didn't love you.

I sent a little message to jean about what just happened :)

7/22/11

How crazy can a guy be? You left me a voicemail saying "I'M GONNA LEAVE YOU" like that isn't awesome!!! I hate you! I loathe you!! You are sooooooo ugly, too, compared to the hot fucking sexy, ripped, single parents and doctors that I have been flirting with lately. The only girl that would go out with you would need to be pretty crazy!!! Once I realized that I could just go talk to people I realized just how many people were wishing that I would!! YOU SUCK in EVERY way. You are a HORRIBLE FATHER and you know you are. LAME. SKINNY. UGLY. BROKE ALL THE TIME. ASKING ME TO TOLERATE YOUR UGLY FACE AND STINKY BODY. HAHAHAHAHA

NOTE: These next few posts were emails exchanged between Kay and another man, and then they were forwarded to me by Kay.

From: ******

To: Kay

Sent: Friday, July 22, 2011 4:45 PM
Subject: Re:

i feel ya....hey you wanna talk on the phone or something?/ i wanna be there for you right now and show you that tough guys do have feelings. I'm a softy. Especially for you.

On Fri, Jul 22, 2011 at 4:56 PM, Kay wrote:

I would love to but my phone was broken a few hours ago

From: **********

To: Kay

Friday, July 22, 2011 4:58 PM
Subject: Re:

that sucks you are such a cool chick to talk to.......So since you're busy today, what do you think of meeting sunday or something?? Getting a drink maybe?? I already KNOW i have to see you this weekend and it seems right to me for some reason...

On Fri, Jul 22, 2011 at 4:59 PM, Kay wrote:

I will meet up with you one of these nights :)

FROM:

TO:

Message flagged

Friday, July 22, 2011 5:02 PM

Message body

awww i'm excited!!! lol Well sunday would be awesome because i don't have anything going on so if you can make it happen you'll be pleasantly surprised. I personally think you deserve to be treated like a queen at least once ya know?? Plus, you KNOW you need a backrub to get rid of all that built up tension.....Tension is BAD for you!!!! lol So what city do ya live anyway?? i'm in bloomington

7/22/11

THIS WILL NEVER HAPPEN AGAIN. NO CONTACT EVER AGAIN. NO KIDS. NO CONTACT WITH ANY OF US BECAUSE YOU ARE FUCKING CRAZY. MY LANDLORD SAYS YOU ARE NOT ALLOWED HERE EVER AGAIN AND MY BRO IS COMING TO WATCH THE KIDS WHILE I GO GET A RESTRAINING ORDER

7/22/11 *Me:*

Yeah? Restraining order for what? Trying to get away from u n getting stabbed in the back of the head? I asked u to leave me alone many times. Before n after u gashed my head open. Bring on the feather man tho. Im still down ---------- Sent from AT&T's Wireless network using Mobile Email

7/22/11

umm, you busted into my house and stole my phone and broke it, you idiot!! You know I don't even like you and have only been letting you hang around out of pity! YOU FUCKING IDIOT. I AM GETTING REIMBURSED FOR THAT PHONE YOU FUCKING ASSHOLE. You just lost all future contact with your daughter because you are a violent fucktard. I have your beard trimmer though.

By the way, all guys take me seriously. They all want to keep me because I'm way smarter and way easier to talk to than anyone around here :)

The featherweight makes you look like a crooked back bitch. I've been telling everyone about you!! I'm getting a restraining order against you for Molly, too, since you busted in the house VIOLENTLY when I begged you to get the fuck out and DUMPED OUT HER MILK like a total PRICK!!!

NOBODY IN THE WORLD CARES, ABOUT YOU, JOE. I JUST GOT DONE TALKING TO JORDAN AND HE DOESN;T REALLY LIKE YOU EITHER!!! NEITHER DOES JEAN!!! Me and the kids were the only ones and now we hate you because you keep KICKING ME AND BREAKING MY STUFF LIKE A PSYCHO!

yOU CAN'T HELP IT? rAISED BY ANIMALS? Just kill your damn self!!! I will make sure you get arrested for this, and I will make damn sure you cant get into the military. Amy has a phone full of pictures from last time and I will GET YOU FOR ABUSING ME.

How can you call me abusive when I beg you to please stop trying to go out with me and just be a good, solid weekend dad? I loathe you and you know I'm seeing other people who are way better than you! How can you say I am abusive when I BROKE UP WITH YOU IN JANUARY AND HAVE BEGGED YOU TO LEAVE FOR MONTHS!!!!

I can get a hot mma fighter here with a 6 inch tongue here in my bed any time I want. he's begging me to just let him eat my pussy with NOTHING in return :)

NOTE: what she is talking about here was a time where she again dumped me for another guy because she was convinced that I was cheating on her, so I asked if I could come get my stuff out of her place. She said that I could come over and I did. I knocked on the door and she let me in and said that I could get my stuff and go. I grabbed my things then I grabbed my milk out of the fridge and dumped it, it was mine, I bought it the night before and I didn't want to be used. I was already paying child support to her and it was more than enough weekly for her to pay for diapers, food, and about half of her rent. On my way out I grabbed a phone that I had also just bought a few days prior and I broke it in half. It was on the counter and not in the middle of a 911 call. I then started for the door, Kay was right behind me punching me and clawing at me. I made it all the way to the alley before she grabbed my beard trimmer out of my hand and I said keep it. She then stabbed me in the back of the head with it and I lunged forward and turned just in time to see her mid swing for my face with the beard trimmer again, I dropped my weight and threw a kick which landed on her leg, which she injured a few days prior, I didn't go for the leg intentionally because I knew it was already injured, I didn't have any time to think I just acted and likely in a manner that may have saved my life. I clearly acted in self defense, I stopped her from wounding me further by using less force than she inflicted on me and then ran away. There was a blood trail for two blocks back to my car, and the blood was from my head, not her "mortally wounded leg". I never wanted to strike a woman but I was in a situation where I needed to react and I am glad that I reacted the way that I did, otherwise I could have died, or been mutilated. The only think I regret is not just leaving her with the phone. Also she said, "I BROKE UP WITH YOU IN JANUARY AND HAVE BEGGED YOU TO LEAVE FOR MONTHS!!!! " but as the above text and dates state she broke up with me then asked me to return and then repeated. I was not stalking or harassing her in any way yet somehow in her mind that's the way that she sees it. And as far as the phone goes I said she could use it temporarily but I intended on taking it back to resell it. It wasn't a gift, it was a loan.

NOTE: These next few posts were also emails exchanged between Kay and another man, and then they were forwarded to me by Kay.

From: ******

To: Kay

Sent: Friday, July 22, 2011 3:21 PM
Subject: Re:

Well that really sucks....Mental abuse they say is worse then physical.....I feel bad.....You know it's something you can overcome if you know how.....Back in highschool, i was a really shy guy, but i met one of my girlfriends and she really helped me get out of my shell and i was all good after that. I think what you need is a guy who'll please you for once.....How good would it be to have a handsome guy (AHEM!!) who'll let you have an experience you won't forget. I have a 6 inch long tongue!! I think if you experience just you getting pleasure, you'll slowly can out of your shell and be more outgoing.....Hmmmmm You know if you want i can do that and you wouldn't have to do anything for me.......Matter of fact i have free time today and tommorrow.....i'm open to the experience if you are...

7/22/11

On Fri, Jul 22, 2011 at 4:21 PM, Kay wrote:

Well thank you. That actually sounds kind of nice. But really, I don't even know you that well. I have only met you like three times Kinda weird. I got drunk last night. Maybe I should have called you then. I'm really, really uptight... Also really really undersexed.

7/22/11

FROM SOME GUY:

well technically how well do ya know anyone ya know...Think about your exes.....You thought you knew them, but look at them now....Besides, when you're uptight, you need that relaxation to start the weekend. I'm even just willing to please you and that's it no sex.....I also gotta admit i give the best backrub ever!!.......Could you spare an hour today?

7/22/11

lol to the compete and lose thing. You go for fat girls on craigslist. I am awesome, and loveable. Brian is a great great friend to me and he makes me feel very safe and happy. There are many reasons why I "don't want to be with him" or whatever, but mostly because I don't need to rope people like you do. YOU FUCKED UP because YOU WERE RAISED WRONG!! Lots of people take me seriously!!

7/22/11

And I love how you psycho schizoids make such a spectacle. You pretend that YOU got over ME hahaha. I fist kissed you into not caring about me anymore? HAHAHAHAHAHAHA!! YAY!! FINALLY!!! THE CRAZY VAN STALKER HAS STOPPED CARING!!! WOOO HOOO!!! ON TO TRY TO RUIN THE LIFE OF JEAN AND ANYONE IN THE WORLD WHO WILL HAVE YA,

Hahahaha you are hanging out with that black drug dealer from outside or you're driving to Jordan hahahaha. SO LAME!!!

7/23/11

You are the worst father and worst boyfriend I have ever had.

7/23/11

I am going to get you thrown in prison. You broke into my house, attacked me, destroyed my property, and I HAVE WITNESSES!! I am pressing charges this time and I am not going easy on you any more. You will get what you deserve now, you woman beater.

NOTE: there were no witnesses to me doing anything immoral or illegal. Her landlord heard me yelling at her to leave me alone while she was attacking me and some guy on the street saw me running away from her and she was screaming for him to stop me, and that I attacked her and so I just waved my blood soaked hand at him that I was holding my head wound with and he just laughed and went about his business.

7/23/11

You are going to get raped in jail. I will get you for this. You will not get away with what you did to me yesterday. Just because I'm seeing other people DOES NOT GIVE YOU THE RIGHT to break into my house, dump out your daughter's milk, break my phone, and kick me in my hematoma 5 times!! YOU ARE SOOOOO CRAZY!!! All of my friends know about the things you do to me and my family knows, too. EVEN MAVEN can testify. I know you said you were leaving the kids (Trying to pretend it was YOU who was doing the dumping HAHAHA!) but you will regret it someday and you have lost the right to be a father.

7/23/11

Ummm somebody couldn't get me off last time..... It really would be nice to have hot sex with a hot guy who knows his way around a pussy instead of a tard like you who needs all these instructions and still sucks at it

7/23/11

liar!!! LIAR!! YOU WERE NOT WELCOME IN HERE AND YOU INTERFERED WITH MY 911 CALL!!! YOU ARE CRAZY IF YOU BELIEVE ANY OF THIS. YOU WILL PAY, AND I WILL PRESS CHARGES FOR ALL OF THIS!!! Amy has all the pictures from all the major beatings and you will pay for all of it.

And one guy is enough for me. I just haven't had one since january when I dumped you, lamer. I never cheated on ya. I just let you weasel your ugly body back into my house a few times when you were acting all honeymoon phase. The past few weeks I have realized that the only way for me to get a new dude with you around all the time would be to lie to you since you thought you were my bf or something. Gotta do what you gotta do when you have a crazy freak stalking you.

7/23/11

Stop responding then, ugly. I'm a great hard working student mother and you torture and abuse me. You are fucked up and you will be incarcerated so you cannot hurt me again. This is my last email to you. Do not respond, ugly guy. Your phone says it doesn;t want to see your ugly meth tooth mouth anymore.

NOTE: I don't have a "meth tooth" I have a filling that fell out of a molar. I have pretty nice teeth.

7/23/11

f9* 64/I would be doing a lot better if I pressed charges in Tucson.. You have definitely relinquished the right to be a father! You don't give a damn about the kids and you told me this MANY times. You ruin my life time and time again... You broke the phone and I lost all of my clients phone numbers. People I will never see again becaue of you. You have fucked me over SO many times and burned so many bridges for me. If you loved those kids you wouldn't hurt their mother.

I wouldn't have to lie to get you in jail, and the fact that you deny the abuse is extra fucked. If you just don't want to admit it because you think it will ssomehow help you in court you are forgetting the long messages you sent Amy where you admitted to pushing me and cried about how sorry you were. She printed them and has been begging me to let her come with me to the cops for 6 months or so. I hate you so much, Joe. I hope you hold your head in your hands and cry. You have been drunk for two weeks and that is where half of your money goes. You need to be locked up. You can't just bust into my house and kick me right in my seriously injured leg multiple times and break my phone while I call 911!! YOU NEED TO LEARN!! You need to be put away so that you can't get drunk and hurt someone else. You will probably come after me next time you are drunk. I know you stalked Troy like a crazy man, too, and I will tell the cops about that, too. You lost your father rights. After I get to the hospital tonight and talk to the cops upon entry you will not hear from me again because I am getting a restraining order and I WANT JUSTICE FOR EVERY TIME YOU PUT YOUR HANDS ON ME or BROKE MY STUFF or cut me down and called me a slut and a stupid bitch. I HATE YOU!!!! WHY COULDN'T YOU HAVE JUST LEFT ME ALONE??? A real man would have said "I'm leaving so I can;t hurt you guys anymore" but you just wont go away and wont stop drinking and driving and fighting and ahhhhhh. The only way to get rid of you is to go full on legal. I should have done it a long time ago. I wouldn't feel like my leg is full of broken glass right now if I wasn't so damn nice to a psychopath

NOTE: I don't know if it constitutes "stalking" but there was a guy, troy, on the internet that was sending me messages about Kay begging for him to satisfy her sexually and frankly he was very offensive and rude. He even said that if he saw me he was going to shoot me and he called me a skinny bitch and things like that. So I used public access websites to figure out who he was and where I could find him. I found out a lot about him and one of the things I found out was that he had health problems, so even though I had his address, phone number, picture, and employment info I decided to let things pass so that I didn't accidentally kill him while I let our conflict play itself out. I do not search out violence and in most cases I will avoid violence but this guy was harassing me for weeks and I figured he would probably just apologize if I stood face to face with him. But again, if it didn't play out like that, I didn't want it to go too far so I did not pursue our meeting. I personally do not think that it constitutes stalking since all I did was obtain public knowledge.

7/23/11

You cut yourself when you were strongarming me and stealing my phone while holding your razor, you dumbass. You know I don't hit you and you know you are the abusive one. You know I am a victim and you just want to make me mad by acting like YOU are a victim. I'm going to the hospital because when you kicked me in the alley you hurt me really bad and there is bruise pouring down my leg from my hematoma. I want justice for this. It feels like broken glass and the lortab isn;t helping at all. We have documented many of these events and you have abused me for too long! You don't get to be alone!! You don't get to not be somebody's prison bitch!! You don't deserve to escape to another state after what you did to me and you are so CRAZY to not realize how horrible it was!!! I was just putting on makeup in the bathroon when yo busted in and I tried to call the cops but you INTERRUPTED MY 911 CALL WITH A

KICK TO THE ARM THAT WAS HOLDING THE PHONE!!!!
MY LANDLORD HEARD IT ALL, AND DUSTIN DOWN
THE STREET WATCHED YOU SMASH MY PHONE AND
DRIVE OFF!! You gave that phone as a gift so that gives you
no right to barge in and attack me while I am calling 911 just
to get the phone back! You don't have friends or family or a
girlfriend so blah blah blah to that. How can you say those
are lies??? YOU TOTALLY DID ALL THAT!!!

I can't believe how many years you took from me and you
can't even be sorry for this. I've been so mad but now I am
just crying because you are so evil and I totally believed in
you for so long. Everybody was so right.... I have 6 months of
your apologies and now that my dad shunned me you just
went right back to abusing me but the frequency increased
and now there is no honeymoon phase in between and no
apologies

7/23/11

And I can't get those numbers transferred and you hurt me
really bad this time!! My leg is green and hot and itchy and it
hurts soooo bad. Why would you do something so serious? It
hurts so bad!!! I just lost the phone? How about I lost all of
my work contacts and it's gonna take me several more weeks
to heal my leg now!! I was not hitting you and you should
really just shut up about that. YOU PROMISED YOU
WOULD STOP HURTING ME AND THIS IS THE WORST
INJURY I HAVE EVER HAD!!! How can you live with this??
Why??? WHAT IS WRONG WITH YOU??? WHY DID YOU
DO THIS TO ME???

7/23/11

There is no point to any of this.... You don't have a soul. If
you don't realize what you have done then you are more

twisted than I ever thought possible. It scares me so bad when I think about how I slept next to you for so long and believed in you for all those years. You promised I would be safe but you don't even feel bad for any of this. You are a monster. Dexter should get you.

NOTE: in this email you can see that she is projecting the realization of her twisted mind onto me. Somewhere in her mind she knows that she did attack me. She knows that I've done many things to keep her safe and because of this attack I refused to return back to her to keep her safe and keep her from impulsive self-destructive ideas and actions. She is hurt that I refuse apologize for her actions and the way that she escalated the situation into a physical one. What she wanted and what I did up to this point, was for me to set aside my feelings and convince her that I was at fault for the situation and beg for her forgiveness. But this was one of the last times that I would let her treat me this way and I refused to accept a fault that wasn't my own and I refused to beg for the opportunity to be abused again.

7/23/11

How about give me a new phone and tell me where you are going?

7/23/11

I never hurt you at all. I tried to get my phone back because I REALLY REALLY REALLY needed it, but I just got hurt really really bad in the process. It is swollen double size and it is green, surrounded by hot hot red, and itchy. As soon as my brother comes I'm rushing to the ER

7/23/11

The legal way to get your dumb ass beard trimmer back would be to ask for it, and then if that doesnt work call the cops to help you. It is never okay to BREAK INTO A GIRL'S HOUSE

7/23/11

How do you expect me to feel right now? Isolated and without a phone. Scared that I am going to need my leg amputated and just waiting, hoping that my family will help me. Shaken up from this terrible week. I just want to be a normal girl.... I am good inside. I am better than most people. I try to do the right thing always. Why did you do this to me?

7/23/11

I DIDN'T TOUCH YOU!!! How can you be so deluded?? You totally must have done that to yourself

7/23/11

you liar!!! You just want to make me mad!!! I did NOT SAY IT WAS OKAY!!! i LOCKED MYSELF IN YM ROOM AND CALLED 911 BUT I HEARD YOU MESSING WITH MY STUFF SO I CAME OUT AND YOU STARTED

THREATENING TO TELL MY LANDLOARDS BAD THINGS
ABOUT ME!!! you are so horrible!!! How

can you live with yourself!!!! I hate you, Joe!! I hate you so
much it is painful!!!

7/23/11

I have been saying that for weeks but now that you mortally
wounded me and I'm afraid I need this thing amputated...
NOW you have gotten the ultimate get back on me and I
have nothing.... I have to take care of the kids like always
with a totally frazzled mental state and find all new clients
and possibly be in a wheelchair.... Now you want me to just
let it go??? I begged you to leave and now you ruined my life
and you expect me to just forget about it? Things would have
been so different if I had just picked a normal guy

NOTE: her leg was fine by the way. It was not amputated
and her career as a physical trainer and exercise instructor
has continued.

7/23/11

I fucking hate you and I always always will/ If you ever grow
a soul you will realize the truth/ I was crying/ I was begging
and saying please/ You are so evil/ I will never forgive you/
One day you will really wish you didnt do this to me/ You
didnt deserve this family

7/23/11

61

Well you must have done that to yourself because I never hurt you/ How bout you put some damn money in my bank account since your overdrawn account took all of my money last week? I put my anytime fitness check in my account and it just went to that overdraft They said I can petition to be taken off the account on monday but I lost that money/ Now I am a severly severly injured single mom with no money and no phone/

7/23/11

I put into my account but they garnished it

7/25/11

Why did you have to do this to me? I'm signing both of the kids over to Tim's family and killing myself this weekend

You ruined my life

7/25/11

yes

7/25/11

Can you put it in my car? You know money would really help too

I wish you weren't so crazy

I loved you very much but you scare me too bad

That is what I was trying to tell you in the nicest ways I could but you never listened

7/25/11

I'm leaving in 8 minutes...... I don't want to see you

did you do it yet?

7/27/11

Stop talking to Derek about me!

I fucking hate you! JUST GO AWAY!

7/27/11

He says you told him I am mean.

Really mature

7/28/11

So are you going to put money in my account or what?

7/28/11

I need diapers you fucking asshole. They took 67 dollars to go to your stupid debt. Tim doesn't give me any money and you are homeless because you are an idiot. I don't want it anymore anyway. Fuck you

7/28/11

DIAPERS IS WHAT I WANT

Anything else would just be wonderful

Diapers are the goal

7/28/11

okay fine just no more talking

I accidentally gave the diapers to the daycare and didn't prepare for this

It was a tiny oversight. I thought I had more

You are one to talk about saving money

7/29/11

You act like Tim

Just trying to press my buttons because you're a bitch

7/30/11

I treated you way too god for a few years you know

but okay whatever you want. I feel better now and I will not talk to you

7/31/11

My cousin who lives in woodbury is having a birthday tonight

Would you watch the kids?

Also Mav needs a haircut soon and I was wondering if you would do the honors

Taking him in to great clips I mean

7/31/11

I have a babysitter so it is okay

I don't know where you are so I don't know about the kids going there

Let me know about the haircut

8/1/11 *me:*

Im glad that u feel better now. I know youre over me. And i just want to get along for the sake of the kids. I will contribute finantially to help with the kids still. I hope u enjoy the rest of your weekend.

8/2/11

Okay I feel super depressed

Could you please come over? I could give you some gas money. I always feel way more calm when you are around

8/2/11

I know you might not get this but I really hope you do. I know you are dangerous and all that but my self esteem is that bad to where I would hang out with somebody who hurts me and tries to provoke me into fighting so he can feel more justified when hitting me. I am just having a bad night I guess. If you could bring me some weed too I will pay you for that and help you out with gas. If I can't get you to come over then I will have to accept the company of people that just want to screw me anyway and that

will make me more sad

8/3/11

Okay so I don't feel sad anymore but I am very horny and can't sleep and I really wanna have sex

I could do it another night but if you could be sober I think we could have a good day together

I haven't been with anybody else but you and if you are clean and haven't been screwing hookers or anybody else then we should help eachother out once

8/3/11

Woah I take all that back

I just remembered brazilcupid and I don't want your little wanker dick

8/5/11

I didn't screw anybody. I did hang out with a few guys and it has made me very very sad

8/5/11

Don't you have a job? I haven't had sex with anybody. I let someone give me a massage and that's it. I kept all of my clothes on and was very rude about it. I just wish he would go away because I know he

would never love me and I just want to be loved

8/5/11

It made me sad because now I realize that you never loved me. You were just using me for stability and housing and a little self esteem boost while you continued to chat with whores. I realize now that you were never totally honest about it and I feel very very bad that I blindly loved you

Sent on the Sprint® Now Network from my BlackBerry®

8/5/11 *Me:*

Oh dont be sad, I wasn't using u and I did love you. Did it hurt when he bit u

8/5/11

I just didn't want the kiss to begin with so it bothered me and he did bite way too hard to be sweet.

8/5/11 *Me:*

Why do u say u wish he would go away? Is he bothering you

8/5/11

He bothers me all the time. He was drunk in my neighborhood so I let him stay on the couch bc he was begging. He didn't want to drive drunk. Then at 6 AM he came in and started massaging me and he kept asking me to take clothes off and I wouldn't do it. I told him to go before the kids woke up and he said "I wanna meet them!"

I told the mav that he was trying to sleep in a garbage can so I was letting him in as a charitable act. Mav thought that was funny and made fun of him for awhile. He asked me to walk him out when he left and forcefully kissed me and bit me

8/5/11 *Me:*

Who is this guy? At least he didnt go any further. Dont let guys sleep in ur place. You have to think about the kids before drunk acquaintances.   Y did he know where u lived? Thats funny that mav made fun of him. Idk about creeps meeting my kids... So what little butt n boob rubbing / spooning

8/5/11

He was on the couch before that and I didn't want him to meet the kids either but he thinks I'm gonna be his new girlfriend soon or something. So he was insistant. He just rubbed down my arms and legs and feet and everything in great detail and told me to try to sleep. The kids woke up at 8 I have hung out with him three times before so he knew where I lived.

8/5/11 *Me:*

Ahh. Where did he bite you? Is he the feather weight? Or mr. 6" tounge?

8/5/11

He bit my lips and he is neither of them. It doesn't matter though because I don't want any of them and I am very sad

8/5/11 *resent*

Okay so I don't feel sad anymore but I am very horny and can't sleep and I really wanna have sex

I could do it another night but if you could be sober I think we could have a good day together

I haven't been with anybody else but you and if you are clean and haven't been screwing hookers or anybody else then we should help eachother out once

8/5/11 *Me:*

I havent had sex with anybody. Ive been sleeping most of the day. I really hope u havent been fucking people...

8/5/11

Can you smoke some weed with me please? I haven't had it for days and I have been to depressed to go get some

8/5/11 *Me:*

If ur just playing me for weed please be honest about it tho. I cant take much more of the games

8/5/11

Nope. I'm lonely. I could play anyone for weed. But I don't want to see you unless you are stone cold sober

8/5/11 *Me:*

When will u be home? Or when should i come over?

8/5/11

I'm home now. But wait... Have you had anything to drink today?

8/6/11

Hey mol is getting sweaty n mad...

8/6/11

Help me please!!!

8/6/11

Hey
Btw remember that I always loved you but your cheating and drinking and beating me are the reasons why I am single and suffering. I hate being alone but you care so little and show no remorse and continue to drink and show that you don't love me even a tiny bit and that jacking off is all that you

really want in life Why? I'm screwed right now and I need your help so hopefully you can save me here

8/6/11

Not only am I totally screwed but I am suffering from a huge hole in my heart. I wanted just two hours of nice just to stop me from reeling and searching like this for just one day... You gave me two hours of watching you stare at random unsuspecting girls and talking to me like I'm trashy.

8/7/11 *Me:*

Kay im concerned. Will u tell me what happened? And wether or not ur ok?

8/7/11
Hey. Do you have minutes on your phone?

8/7/11 *Me:*

No i dont. Why are u screwed kate? U should tell me whats up.

8/7/11

I'm driving and I'm okay now

8/7/11 *Me:*

Heeeello? Ur phone is back on u wanna let me know whats up?

8/7/11

Don't be mean. I love you

8/7/11 *Me:*

Im sorry, i wasnt trying to sound mean, i just wanted to know what was going on. I was worried.

8/7/11

I know. I will tell you when I can. Its okay now

8/7/11

Will you come over tonight?

8/8/11

Come stay with me

8/8/11

We have no money and no diapers and we need you

8/8/11

I have no diapers and no money! Help meeee

8/8/11

Get over here!

8/8/11

Please pick up mav!!! I need you with the damn family! Why are you not here?

8/8/11

Please grab some diapers from Molly's classroom. Please Joe

8/8/11 *Me:*

Well i did just get done w work n as far as i knew diaper money was the objective. Dont get mad at me.

8/8/11

I'm not mad. I'm sorry. Are you there yet?

8/8/11

I'm starting to panic. Are you gonna help us or what? Please answer me!

8/8/11

Did you get him yet? The news is scaring me

8/8/11 *Me:*

5 mins whats the key code?

8/8/11

**** pound key

8/9/11 *Me:*

So did u get molly into daycare today?

8/9/11

I did. How are you doing?

8/9/11

I got the foodstamps back

8/9/11 *Me:*

Im okay. I breathed in too much polyoximethelene (acetal) dust today tho. Nasal passage feels numbish, lungs are burning, but somehow its non toxic plastic?

8/9/11

Oohhhh scary. At least we can do food therapy?

8/9/11 *Me:*

How about u? How are u?

8/9/11

Mad paperwork plus tired

8/9/11 *Me:*

Very nice. New card?

8/9/11

Yes. I rode my bike down there to get it

8/9/11 *Me:*

Tell the paper work to lighten up n smile! Haha. Just passed up a twins game w the owner here. So i can c u guys instead :)

8/9/11

Thanks bebe. I'm glad we get to see you

8/9/11 *Me:*

Prob not til like 6ish tho... Gotta dig thru that dudes shit to get pawnables. Also we can return some stuff i bought maybe

8/9/11

Sex

8/9/11 *Me:*

Huh? Yes please, elaborate tho?

8/9/11

My p*ssy wants it

8/9/11 *Me:*

I want that p*ssy

8/9/11

Its ready right now

8/9/11 *Me:*

So can ur pussy wait until 5?

8/9/11

It will have to. It's gonna feel good when we get to it, though. I'm pretty much as ready as I can get for waiting in a line at half price books

8/9/11 *Me:*

Hmmm... Okay? Why the bookstore?

8/9/11

They take movies

8/9/11 *Me:*

K driving. C u in 35 mins

8/9/11

Ok love you

8/10/11

Tell me whats going on kate.

8/10/11

Whaaat?

8/10/11 *Me:*

So what else arent u telling me then? Please be honest with me

8/10/11

How about some honesty from you for once

8/10/11

You should be glad that I told you instead of not telling you. You are kind of an ass. You just shun me because of my act of kindness towards you? Its not like I owe you anything

8/10/11

Also you reminded me that you are not a good man and that I need to look out for myself and get away. You really aren't. You are unkind and treat me poorly. I have a conscience and wanted to be nice and boost your self esteem for the long road ahead. We can visit you every other weekend but just please don't follow us

8/10/11

But you act like a fuckhead and beat me up and break my phones! You were going to abandon them and flee the cops! You don't deserve the kids that easy! You had us and you lost us! I'm leaving because of you! You need to get rid of that entitlement bullshit

8/10/11

Seeing the kids is not your right.

8/10/11

You aren't even sorry when you hurt me anymore so I have to find a new role model for them

8/10/11

That's really creepy that you could write that when I know you did some pathetic sexting shit and lied about it. Be honest with me for once.

8/10/11 *Me:*

I am not a bad man n u know it.

8/10/11

You treat me pretty bad every fucking day

8/10/11

I just wanna finish college and get married. I have 25 credits left

8/10/11 *Me:*

And yesterday u said that u love me. U said i was the best guy. I didnt shun u, i was hurt. I hate this kay.

8/10/11

I was telling you that so you could remember it in the coming months alone in your hotel room. I figured it would make you feel better. I always tried to boost your confidence while you always tried to make sure I have none

8/10/11

I didn't say you were the best guy though. I said I loved you but you are a bad, cruel man who can't treat me well

8/10/11

Sorry to have interupted ur morning. I deserved that explosion of insults n cruleness

8/10/11

I wasn't cruel. I woke up to you bitching at me because I spoke the truth. Don't try to make me think I am bad because my heart is good. That is all.

8/10/10

You can't say I broke your heart either because I invited you in to see the kids and have affection for one more week before I really leave. We weren't talking at all before that

8/10/11

Hey, can you pick up the kids today? I have that power bar class at the sweatshop at 530

8/10/11 *Me:*

Yeah. Thought it was at 6.

8/10/11

It is from 530 to 630 I think

8/10/11 *Me:*

Didnt mean to b a dick. Sorry.

8/10/11

Finally realized you wanted something of mine? What is it?

8/10/11

As long as you got to act shameful in front of my son and give him crazy stepdad memories and call me a few names now you can give me a weak ass "I'm sorry's" you now think you have done enough bad to keep the king douchebag crown. Good for you

8/10/11

You do it to yourself, thickskull!

8/10/11

Why did you ever pretend to be a nice guy if you are just going to be a stoneface stubborn asshole to me forever?

 I didn't want a boyfriend and you tricked me

8/11/11

Can you watch music videos?

8/11/11

Hello?
Meet at home?

8/12/11 *Me:*

What u up to?

8/12/11

Just about to buy a beverage. I love you :)
I have a good idea for what we can do this afternoon if you
have time

8/12/11 *Me:*

And whats that?

8/12/11

We can ride our bikes around that whole grand rounds thing
or we can try an awesome fitness class for free

8/12/11 *Me:*

Im down for biking.

8/12/11

Don't drink any alcohol if you wanna hang out with me
today, okay?

8/12/11 *Me:*

Yep. No booze

8/12/11

Or beer!

8/12/11 *Me:*

Whaaaat!? Haha yeah just wild cherry pepsi

8/12/11

NO POP EITHER!!!

8/12/11 *Me:*

what will u be doing in around an hour?

8/12/11

Waiting for you? Can you come faster than that?

8/12/11 *Me:*

Yeah ill try. Packing up my stuff here. Then im outta here

8/12/11

Where are you?

8/12/11

Hey! I want to go home! Where are you?

8/15/11 *Me:*

Got an interview at dingwells at 10 am tomorrow again haha. Hows ur morning going?

8/15/11

We're all holding hands walking to the park right now. That's great!! I got a little more done but a few more bags and boxes would help

8/15/11

Ahhh I keep having dark thoughts about how I'm probably born to die since my mother thinks I'm wretched. Ahhhhh

8/15/11 *Me:*

Boxes n bags huh? Poop. They sell them instead of give them away here in the cities... What park u going to?

8/15/11

The playground daycare was in session so we're taking the car and going somewhere

8/15/11 *Me:*

Nice. That one out on snelling is nice...

8/15/11

I'm at the one by edgecumbe and highway 5

8/15/11

If we can just make it to suptown we don't have to come back... Even if your car died. You can stay with me if you need to

8/15/11 *Me:*

Okay. Its not dying as much as its falling apart tho. I love u so much

8/15/11

I love you, too!!!
Love you love you and just can't wait to see you later

8/15/11 *Me:*

Wow that was really nice

8/15/11

I'm going crazy Ahhhhh
My mom is such a bitch
And peter is an idiot! I need to see you to calm me down ahhhh

8/15/11 *Me:*

Im sorry. Ill b a little late today. Gotta change a tire

8/15/11

Changing a tire for a girl..... Great

8/15/11
We're all waiting for you to try to get the phone number. Just give her your screen name and help us pack this shit up please. It has been a bad enough day already! Come on! Please just tell her to call triple A?? I can't believe you. You know I regard this as cheating

8/15/11
In going crazy!!! Can one person come through today??? Fuck! We have to hurry!

8/15/11

come on come on don't do this to me

8/15/11

Still not coming????????????

8/15/11

Could you be decent and call me at least?

8/15/11 *Me:*

Changing my tire... N dont call me a girl haha

8/15/11

I'm sorry!!!!!! I'm not meant to be a stay at home mom!!!! This day is jamaican me crazy!!!
We have big trouble to talk about. Hurry home please

8/15/11 *Me:*

Kate this has to be fixed. its not my fault I got a flat.

8/15/11

Omg it's not done yet??? AAAAAAHHHHHHH

8/16/11

Love u too

8/16/11

I'm ready when you are

8/16/11 *Me:*

Tried calling. Going to the library

8/16/11

I'm at angelas house!

8/16/11

Playing with the neglected kids. Wanna leave soon?

8/17/11

Oh the St thomas bookstore buyback is this weekend.
I love you

8/18/11 *Me:*

Just met one of those bums! Haha he was looking for his needles!

8/18/11

What's up?
Tim has been yelling at me all night because I asked about child support again

8/18/11

Hey, can you tell me how you're doing?

8/18/11

Waaaah worst day ever. Come back please

8/18/11

On my way. I will call you in a bit

8/18/11

On my way to you

8/18/11

Just bringing molly. Also have a mooch with me

8/18/11

Still not even close. Would you get some weed pleeeease?

8/18/11

A little. Tried and failed at plasma donating

8/18/11

Why? Doing sonething bad?

8/18/11

Any weed bebe?

8/18/11

I love you btw
Molly is awesome

8/18/11

Not long. What are you doing?

8/18/11

Probably getting there at ten

8/18/11

Bruce is with me btw

8/18/11

I hate you

8/18/11

Realizing that you will always be mean to me and hating you

8/18/11

Even in front of people... Just bad upbringing I guess. I learned a lot recently......

8/18/11

Don't care what you say. Still know I deserve at least one rung better and never stopped hating you. Weed plz?

8/18/11

What?

8/18/11

Will you PLEASE pick us up at o garas??? Plzzzz we are. Drunk!! Please?

8/18/11

Poor baby! Victinm of mine! Maybe go away?

8/18/11

I hate you more than anything. Leave my house. I hope you die.

8/18/11

I treated you like crap because you are a crap man. Fucking horriblke woman beater and I would do anything for a better life. I wish I never came down here near you

8/18/11

Well come back and smoke us up pkz???

8/18/11

Come in herE and smoke

8/18/11

Come pon I'm sooo drunk!!!

8/18/11

I'm crying and can't stop please smoke with me

8/18/11

Please comeback

8/18/11

I just wabted nmy keys. Please don't let me cry all night

8/18/11

Not in my heart but yes, I guess so.

8/18/11 *me:*

U bit me pretty hard again.

8/18/11

I guess I am sorry. Just smoke me up please

8/18/11

I'm really drunl and you jave been horrible to me

8/18/11

Actuallt nevernind. You guys choose bc I'm starting to like somebody else and I hate you abyway so bye. Calloing the cops for the keys lata

8/18/11

Crying just ended and crush just re began, fuck you. I hate you. Bye.

8/18/11

Btw I am the ONLY girl who thinks you look okayM. Everyone else says you uglay

8/18/11

And even I don't thinkyou are cute anympore. You know I fake it

8/18/11

As ***** calls it " the Joe life" really does fucking suck and I see that now. No wonder nobody loves you

8/18/11

I unlocked it, horrible guy

8/18/11

Well I just unlocked the doors bur In gonna pass out anyways so do what you do, bitch. My family will get over these hard times and you will not. Fuck you. Come in and apolpgize or go to hell

8/18/11

Hahahhahah okay but nobody ever thought so, EVER.

8/18/11

Hahaha. Every ugly guy let's me boost his ego! I go for ugly guys! Get it through your head! Hahahahaha. Girls laugh at your arms

8/18/11

Stop fuckibg with me wheb inm so drunk bc I will tell you truths you won't forget so easy

8/18/11

I have the truth if you want it

8/19/11

I hate you more than anything and have a fantasy about somebody who will break your neck in a minute. Yay. The end of this poor child nightmare. So glad you weren't faking that you loved me tonight so I can take his dick when I get home

8/19/11

I hate you and don't want you living with me.
The only people who roll their eyes when I talk are jealous bc their stories suck
Just go away if you can't be nice
Hate you

8/20/11

Someone stole the rest of the weed

8/20/11

Fucking ignoring me now? You really are a shitty guy.
Fucking ridiculous

8/20/11 *Me:*

Oh yeah? I wonder who it was. I was sleeping. Chill

8/20/11

Sleeping because your moron ass wasn't sober yesterday? Just keeping on drinking the juice that keeps you insane?

8/20/11 *Me:*

What is ur problem? Ur bro stole ur weed? Y b mean to me bc that?

8/20/11
I'm mean because you were a fucking dick when I came up to spend the night with you. I hate you.

8/20/11

as long as you drink every day and treat women that way, you will never have a good life. I hate you for

shattering everything.

8/20/11

Soooo not invited with me and Danielle tonight

8/20/11

You're a fucking bum and you always will be, bitch. No kids for you today. We're going to the gym and you don't get invited for that either

8/20/11

Ohhh btw I have a date for tonight. I was just now giving you a chance to beg to be my escort tonight but naaahhhh.

8/20/11 *Me:*

Glad to c u had ur daily dose of crazy today. U dont get to tell me what to do. Im single right? U dont get to control my life.

8/20/11
Hahaha do what you want to. It just keeps you poor. Fucking dumb and crazy bummy superior trash. Soooo glad you followed me back so you can be a max failure

8/20/11

Btw I'm just pissed bc I drank that rockstar you gave me and you're a freak

8/20/11 *Me:*

Yeah use the kids as leverage. Classy. Well im drinking today too. Get over it. And have fun being a slutty butt cuz ur mad.

8/20/11

Yes staying craaaaazy!!! It's about time you grew into it

8/20/11

Take your van and find the next willing woman!!! I've been saying that!!!! Either an underage girl who is easily fooled or a shitty nasty hoe. Gotta take what you can get when you are super shitty and crazy chicago street trash. And I just wanna get laid anyway. Haven't been fucked by a full size man in a long time :)

8/20/11

Hahahahahaha yeah right. You just can't afford to live on your own because you're so stupid with your money. Hahahahaha suuuuure. You "love" the kids. Couch surfing at 27. CooOoooool hahahahhaa always will be like that

8/20/11

Danielle thinks you are ugly!!! She always makes fun of me for how ugly you are.

8/20/11

No. I'm hurt bc you were really mean in st paul and I really was excited to see you.

8/20/11

She calls you skinny and hates red hair. Its actually bc of you. I knew you liked to cheat so I was worried you would be checking her out and all that

8/20/11

Just told her what you said. I don't even know why you keep doing this to me. I loved you but you are just so mean and crazy

8/20/11

She said she liked you right up until you said that. She's never fucked a ginger and never will

8/20/11

Not mad that you had fun with two scuzzies acting like trash. I'm mad that you are never gonna be more than a drunk ass bum. That's okay though. Can't save you if you don't need saving. Sky's the limit for me, still. Just gotta say live and let die

8/20/11

Idk I'm just still mad from the can of pop and never got to shoot your head off and release the feelings

8/20/11

Yeah. It wore off a while ago. Now I am just dumbfounded by how much you suck and how fake all that "I've changed, I've grown up" shit was. It's okay though because I still have the whole world ahead of me and good grades that will get me into any grad school so someday me and the kids will have much more than you ever took away from us and the wisdom to stay away from guys like you

8/20/11

Nahhh you are a dick and a perpetual drinker. Everybody everywhere thinks you're a dick except a few people in Superior and people like me and I have a future so f youuuu don't talk to me anymore, I do not care. You will be old and poor soon so better live it up now while you still barely can. Having an awesome day now so not opening any mo of yo shitty emails

8/23/11

Da da da da douchebag!!!
You act like an ass right in front of them!! Do us all a favor
and get drunk and get lost in lake superior or something.
Fuck yew

8/24/11

Btw you being a douchebag is the wedge. Not me. You know I
try, but you are retarded. It is out of my hands.

8/24/11 *Me:*

Kay im not being a douche or drinking. I just want to be
a   da   da   da   dad. We didnt even drink at
the casino btw. We went out there at like 3 am. Just played
21. U act like im drunk all the time n a bad guy but im not. I
took an over $10 an hour pay cut so i could still be around
my daughter, just please let me see my kids kay. Im sorry
that we havent been getting along.

8/24/11
You are SUCH A DOUCHE. I have to get a new email!! My
life is awesome right now don't fuck it up for me again!! Go
aways! Bye byes!!! I will retaliate if you talk to me with police
and everything. I will go public about you bc other people
will get it when they see it live! Use the court for Molly but
your are just insane when you are mad and you made me
hate you so much!! You icky guys left a porn in the baby's
room!! Freaks! Ugh!! I have OPTIONS and you are not one
of them!!! Hate you YOU ARE WAY TOO CRAZY TO BE A
DAD!! Go hang out with underage kids until you turn 30!
You fail!

NOTE: the porn thing was her brother, who was staying with her at the time, I hadn't even been in her house for weeks at this point. And I haven't bought a porn magazine since I was 18 years old. She just didn't want to hold her brother accountable, but later admitted that she knew it was his. And I don't have a single under-aged friend.

8/24/11

Um, everyone will explain how you are a nutso prick stick and she will understand. You were a loony last time they saw you and I'm not going to take any more chances. Already filed to switch to WI so no fraud here. No extortion plz. Throw a can of pop on some other kids mom from now on.

8/24/11

You always have a reason to act like a white trash criminal in front of my kids. Well, bruce brought your brother his bike which was nice of him. you actually said some shit about him being the new dad right in front of the kids. Wow you are fucking dumb. Just a brain full of mush. I tell ya. Do you seriously think bruce is the guy I have in mind? Haaaaa wow. You forget that I have custody and if you want shit from me you better kiss ass, pay child support, be sober, have a real place to live, and not be a douchebag! Sorry. Don't need you. I have plenty of help and friends and I am awesome. I don't want to raise white trash freak kids when I can raise awesome kids like me! Btw Chris told me about the porn, dummy. You be the grown up. I'm the one with jobs, a plan, a stable mind, a rational temper, a good vocab, the ability to not be violent, etc. Fucking crazy!!! Who throws pop on people? A piece of shit disrespectful bastard from chicago, that's who.

NOTE: while this email was really well worded and sounds responsible and mature, it is not. I do not act like a white trash criminal, especially not in front of kids. Bruce is a guy that provokes my anger and what I say to bruce is my business. She stated that I must kiss her ass to be able to see my kids. What is that? She insults me by calling me "fucking dumb." Continuing on to say "just a brain full of mush." Chris guessed that she found a porn when she said youll never guess what I found in the kids room, he didn't actually know for a fact that there was a porn. I have been doing contract jobs where I work 84 hours a week but she insists that shes the one with a job. She claims to have a stable mind, yet openly admits to b.p.d. she claims to have a rational temper but if you've read up to this point you can clearly see that she does not. The ability to not be violent doesn't matter if you are violent. And I'm not from Chicago. So again while it appears to be a well written email it is in fact full of delusion.

8/24/11

How about Shut the fuck up? How about eat shit and die??? Uuuugggghhh. Stop talking to me. Just turn it around and get a fucking therapist. Anybody who is willing to live with you is in for hella trouble bc you are insane. Wait a few fucking months at least, you looney toon. I hate you. Btw Danielle wouldn't fuck you with someone else's pussy. She rolls with guys WAY hotter than you and your ego is based on my stroking it. You aren't as hot as I told you. I always tend to do that with guys hahaha. Go aways freak!

8/24/11

Then don't talk to me because all I want to do is kick your face in until it's all fucked up. Instead I run and work out the anger. Then you push me to talk to you and this is what you get. Hate you buh bye

8/24/11

It does make me happy muwahahahaha I heard you got served too hahahahaha

8/24/11

Cops called looking for ya

NOTE: it was for civil court for unpaid bills to a hospital. Not for criminal activity. And they didn't get ahold of me to serve me a subpoena, but they did still sue me, apparently I was misinformed as to whether or not you could be unknowingly sued, I thought I had a rite to dispute it, but I guess not.

8/25/11

Now is fine. Then I can run to walmart

8/25/11

Hurry! Molly is being adorable and cuddly

8/29/11

I know you did mean to and I already fucking warned you about that today

8/29/11

God dammit. You never learn a fucking thing. You just wrestle for the power to bring me down on a day to day. It's really fucked up. It's like your life purpose or something.

8/29/11

Wow. Abandon the eye rolling fucker that wants to fuck my friends? Who could abandon a guy that lays on the floor and "babysits" and acts like he's some amazing hero for the bare mininum? Get over yourself. Seriously. Roll your eyes in a mirror and you'll wanna punch the reflection bc it is really snotty.

8/29/11

All you fucking do is lay there and you stay there like a big fucking turd when I ask you to do shit. It's like you want to make sure I never start to see potential in you. Just go be fuckhead asshole joe and find the next willing woman because I'm NEVER gonna put up with a slackjawed eyerolling dickhole like you ever again

9/17/11

I never got a text from you so it's okay

9/17/11

The kids are good. If you can stay out of my face and out of MY life you can take molly every other weekend with a few evenings and overnights of your choice. Daycare dropoff and pickup will allow for us to not see eachother. After I see Bruce with his baby I realize that she will be fine as long as we don't talk

9/28/11

Hey, we were talking about every other weekend plus one weeknight of your choice. Did you want the weeknight this week? You can drop her off and pick her up at daycare. Also, Maven does miss you so if you want we could work something out for a little visit or something. Thursdays I work at the Y for just one hour while they go to the daycare. If you want you can see them both for that hour and rest assured that I'm not using you for babysitting while I party or anything

9/28/11

I mean you could pick them up or meet me at the Y and take them for one hour instead of them going to the Y daycare for an hour
I may be training a client at 6 now so it might be two hours but my shift is officially 1 hour long

9/29/11

My phone just died!! Like just went black for no good reason and destroyed my life for a day!! Do you want them tomorrow?

9/29/11

Yeah. When I'm at work. My phone is dead so if you want to take them you can meet me at the MWC whereever my car is parked as I'm leaving power pilates at 4:30. We can go pick them up and I'll show you how. Then youd take them from 5 to 6

9/29/11

Anychance you would get a 10 sack for me? I'd give you 10 dollars and 2 beers for the delivery. I just don't want to waste study time going to get weed

9/29/11

No!! I have no company! I was just studying!!

9/29/11

Wow. I'm sorry. Could you come back? Please?? two beers for ya...

9/29/11 Why would you accuse me of having "nasty company"? That's really not a healthy way to talk to the mother of your kids. Especially since I am sitting here alone memorizing acids and bases and finding

formula masses on the floor

9/29/11

Okay. I will go down there. Jeeze. You're so mean

9/29/11

You are a super fucking asshole and if you think that you are acting normal then I wonder what kind of crummy people you hang out with. I will not ask you again. You could have just said 'No". I was pretty sure you weren't coming and I was fine with that. If I knew I would have to listen to you being a shitty guy then I never would have even let you rain on me with your awful attitude. Forget you

9/29/11

Yeah well people do nice things for me all the time and don't act like you do. You fucking suck! UGH. I fucking hate you

9/29/11

DOUBLE BIRD FUCK YOU!!! How wonderful life is when you're not in the world! Dumb ass reasoning always. You expect me to sit at my email waiting for you to respond? Who does that?

9/29/11

I can get my own shit. I was just doing YOU a favor by giving you something to do! And really, I haven't hung out with Bruce in a month so if that is where you get this idea of me hanging out with "skunky" guys you are sorely mistaken. I can get some pretty hot guys with jobs, muscles, biochem degrees, twin brothers who also have biochem degress and crushes on me, martial artists with amazing personalities.... Fuck. I'm awesome. I have a 6pack now too!! Woo!

9/30/11

You're a shitty dad anyway and I do a better job without you. I think the kids will probably not blame me for excomunicating a freak like you. I DO have a 6 pack. I'm not even sleeping around. Derek broke up with his gf so we hooked up (it was amazing) and now I'm satisfied and ready to scan the world for the next guy with potential for the long term. That's called dating. Just letting guys treat me good and tell me I'm amazing. I have a dinner date tonight and plans every night for the next 4 days. yay   Alright. I'm done. Have fun. Don't retaliate or I will get you back.

9/30/11

lol at the dreams and plans. HAHAHAHA I rock. And roll. ALL night long sweet suzy. My family loves me. You are the one with no family, dopey. When you aren't around to encourage me to I don't fight with them. You suck. I know you'll respond to this because you are like a predictable stupid dog that will always do the same dumb shit. Just gotta make you mad

9/30/11

It's not pointless though because it's fun and funny for me! I hope you respond so I can laugh later. Got done with everything early and worked out really great so I'm gonna enjoy this nice afternoon and go on an afternoon lunch date! Life is so great. Keep it coming stupid dog brain

9/30/11

He went to treatment on Monday thanks to me forcing him to get insurance and setting it all up! All the rest of his friends were indicted in that fed bust! He does love the heck out of me right now! Everyone in my family knows that I'm a strong female and that I am the one who saved Tyler. I started a family fit program here in town and I'm making 8 grand off the first session. Also I only have 13 more credits plus an internship/capstone to do and I'll have a bachelors. A crazy guy patent... Whatever :) Girls don't like broke ass losers who drink a lot and are skinny and ugly and crazy! I doubt they would flirt with you unless they were fat or retarded! Everyone says you look like you have aged 10 years! Hope you make money so you can pay for your kid, you deadbeat piece o shit

9/30/11

That's funny because I have never met a girl who thought you weren't ugly. I always lied to boost your self esteem. Your life is a mistake in the first place and I'm so high above you when not splintered off and isolated by your craziness that NOBODY understands why I ever went out with a loser like you! No women love slim men hahahahahaha wow! You KNOW you're ugly so why are you pretending to think you aren't? Everything you say is the opposite of true and looking at porn and pictures on dating websites doesn't count as meeting flirty girls hahahaha lame

9/30/11

And you're right about me being an intense chick! Ripping you a new one does keep everyone else in the good graces I'm harnessing that energy and using it to kick ass though. Everyone knows I'm a great person though. I had a guy say to me today "I don't care if I ever get into you. You keep providing me with new experiences. I'm on TEAM KAT" I'll be fine as long as I still with submissive guys since I am a dominant type. You just werent my type. I'm still a good person. The longer I go single the better I do at work and school and the more amazing and sexy the puppydogs get

10/1/11

Don't accuse me of being on speed you fucking retard. I ate at erberts and gerberts and famous daves yesterday! You're so retarded!!

10/12/11

Yeah. I do understand it was all overboard. I guess I don't have respect for you but I could try to if you could do that for me once in awhile. You've just been so mean to me for so long and I was always suffering at your hand. It's a defense mechanism because you are so cruel. It's hard though. I'm feeling like I want a boyfriend tonight and I don't want to be like Marilyn Monroe and call somebody just to hold me but I just don't want to be a single mom forever and you are never going to have a house for the kids to stay with you on weekends or anything normal so I need to pick somebody and I hate it

10/12/11

And I did like to make you happy. That's why I always stroked your ego which I think is the only reason that you liked me. I have a bad night like once per month and tonight I am having one. Too much homework and pms and for the first time in months I am chillin by myself and I fucking hate it. Thinking about life and all that. Reading emails. Blah acting impulsively. That's when I email you--When I need to act out of impulse to get through the stress that I'm under.

It's not because I'm crazy and if I was why wouldn't you want to have something to do with Molly? The world is not black and white. Mostly gray. We are in a gray area here where there is no right or wrong... Just two hurt people. Poor kids. What can happen here? Could we stop? I could if you could. You'd really have to stop for real though. No talking about me having "nasty company" and stuff because the minute you get mad I will probably trip out. That's how I react to your jabs now. I know a lot of amazing people and you have no idea what you're saying. I'm a great person and everyone likes me and you used to so please stop trying to ruin my self esteem and maybe I could stop trying to ruin yours. Also do you drink every night? That could be a problem

10/12/11

btw as soon as I get over the jealousy thing I did with Tim and you then I will be a good girlfriend! I think there's that and the body image and I'm getting used to reality more and more and accepting the way life is. You should have listened when I told you that before. Shit. I'll just go wake up Peter. For some reason it feels theraputic to spam you once in awhile. I feel like nobody really knows me all that well anymore and they all just think I'm great and nobody believes me when I say I'm bad news bears. You have done it to me millions of times so don't give me shit for it or I'll start pulling your old emails up. I see some of them on this very page so don't act like life isn;t rough sometimes

10/14/11

You're never seeing her again. Sorry. You're a mess and I see now that you're just like your mother. Better to find a new stepdad and get her used to him.

10/14/11

Okay. It's really selfish of your to abandon me with the kids and drink every day but what can I do?

10/14/11

Stop blaming this on me! I loved you! You were supposed to go to anger management and quit drinking and you never did those things! How can you act like I didn't try to make it work????????????????????????

10/14/11

Look at Mav boxing btw

10/14/11

Also please realize what you are saying. You are saying that you need some time to drink and be violent-- The two problems that destroyed our family and kept making me have to leave you even though I loved you-- before you can come back to your baby daughter? I'm supposed to say "Ohhh okay. You need time away from me and the kids to help yourself get drunker and more violent. Cool. Once you gain all of the gifts that being drunk and violent have to offer then you can have all the time with my precious children that you want!" That isn't helping yourself and I was not the problem! Please put the bottle down

10/14/11

Can you please call me?

10/14/11

You said you have been drinking every day and it sounds like you have already commited many violent acts since we've last been together. I had a great day. I don't know why I feel this way but I'm crying now because I still love you

10/15/11

I do love you and I'm sorry for being mean. You just hurt me a lot. You know you did. I hope you can find some peace and stop hurting yourself

10/15/11

Joe. I don't like Biology anymore. It's boring now. It's making me go insane thinking about doing an internship at the EPA. Jungle boy just texted me and asked me to train at his gym. I have no time. AHHHHHHHHHHHHHHHHHH

10/15/11

It's not a date at all. He has a beautiful pregnant wife. It's all about fitness and being one of the top badasses in the area. The EPA is the environmental protection agency.

10/15/11

I want to open my own gym. I do not want to do biology in any way. I hate it in a sense. I met a guy at the Y who worked there and regrets his biochem degree and physics minor and I know I will too!! WHY DID I DO THIS???????

10/15/11

Uhh I am a little bit of a hypocrite because I got drunker than I have ever been in my life last night and got into a fight. I didn't even plan on drinking but peer pressure got me. My head is killing me and I have that I-got-punched-in-the-face feeling now. I'm going crazy trying to decide what to do about this bio degree problem

10/16/11

I was thinking of switching Spanish major and bio minor and I can go to grad school if I get bored when I'm old or if I break my back. I could even do that half online and at night. I really don't want to work in a lab at all. The internship sounds so boring and I just want more time to box and do yoga and run all day. I discovered how to do this 8 hours per day and turn that into MONEY. Money is what I want. The kids can be right there with me in the gym now. Mav does kickboxing and boxing and has fought with 3 different trainers. The class that we teach is starting next month and he has definition in his calves. Not only that, but I hear "Wow. Molly is BA" or "Molly is a future MMA fighter" all the time. If I go all out studying biology for any fucking longer I am going to miss precious time with my kids and they can be average ass kids who get pregnant young and grow up watching spongebob for hours every day.

10/16/11

I was crying for a little bit then someone came up hee and put on a movie so I sucked it up and fell asleep at 10. Then more people came up here trying to get me to drink a bottle of schnapps and eventually I indulged: Fucking native americans shouldn't drink because this guy started yelling at another guy for "Stealing me away from him" and tried to jump out the window. One guy was hanging onto him and I tried to help but we couldn't pull him back in. I had to sink my teeth into him as hard as I could and he came back in the window because of the pain. Then he socked me in the face twice and he got me down and was on my face trying to choke me out. Raf pulled him off me and threw him out. It was fucked up.

10/17/11

Why are you icing me? I gave you my time for so long after I broke up with you. I'm so compassionate and loved you so genuinely and you just used me for stuff. Then you knock me up, beat me up, leave me and blame it all on me. I'm a person too! If you cried to me you know I'd put my hands on your head and be there for you. Now what am I supposed to do? A couple more very bad things happened to me . I have nobody else to tell and I need to overcome it quickly so I can go get the kids out of bed and have a good day.

10/17/11

It's okay. I have babies and I am strong. I wont talk to you anymore

10/17/11

I left you because you kept hurting us!! Don't you remember how it went down? I loved you always and only left when you were too horrible to stand it. You're mean to the people close to you. Something you learned from Allen? I don't know. Some hippies just blew my mind today and I'm just going through so much philosophical confusion. I'm having a hard time with knowing what is right. I didn 't want drunk timberniggers either. I face pushed that guy and even beat him up once which is why I am not crying about getting beat up by him. I don't want anybody. I think I want to do martial arts or something. I'm pretty BA in the gym and so are the kids. I wish you coud be my friend because you're the last person

that I ever clicked with tht well. I wish somebody else could hold my respect.

10/17/11

Wow. I'm really not doing too good. I just wish we could all sit down together for one night. Do you ever wish that?

10/17/11

For a whole winter you pretended to be sorry and now you just insist that you did nothing wrong? You're a violent alcoholic! I took you to a steely dan concert and you wen t crazy in the morning. You can't even be respectful of your woman for one weekend! Why?? You didn't feel lucky enough for having someone to go to the zoo with and gestate and nurse a child for you? Can't you be nice to me? I'm just a girl and my world doesn't have to be as hard as yours. You try to make it that way but it shouldn't be!

10/17/11

The martial artists and the occupy Duluth hippies are sucking me in. The kids like them too. I'm in a philosophical flux and I'm about to change a whole lot very soon

10/17/11

I'm not doing too good. The kids are not doing good either.

10/22/11

Took the second one right now when Mav wasn't looking

10/23/11

Your daughter got stung by a hornet in bed this morning and is still in the ER. Maven opened the window during the night at some time. Fuck you for ignoring my calls.

10/23/11

I didn't do anything wrong and why would I be fucking my roommate when I have much better options? You must be drunk from the plane. I feel bad for you. There is nothing you could do for Molly anyway. Go ahead and do whatever you need to completely if it helps you mask your pain or whatever.

10/23/11

Hey. You love me. A lot of people do. You know that if you spoke with some respect to the mother of your kids like an adult you would have to see how good I am in a normal mood and then the love would hurt again. You are drinking though so I have no expectations other than you acting foolishly

10/23/11

Hey you can try to guess who I'm banging though haha

10/24/11

Wow you get so mad. So what's the deal with Molly?

10/24/11

I'm sorry you are so mad. I left you a voicemail and I hope you feel better

10/24/11

Sorry.

10/24/11

I can tell you hate me and I guess it is better than what you were doing before. I feel really bad for saying that because you already were so angry and full of hate the past week and now you just seem lost in it. I'm sorry you I ever let you into my intense life. I'll let you out of it. And Tim, too. Go pretend it never happened. Have a good night

10/24/11

I'll block you too so we can't fight anymore

10/24/11

Ahhh can't figure it out but I think you should block me because I know your email has that feature. I flagged you as spam so hopefully that works.

10/24/11 *Me:*

Will do. Have a nice life Kay.

       This was just an account of about six months of emails and texts to my email. In that time I did also receive text messages, phone calls and personal interactions which were all the same. It was very stressful, challenging and tiring to maintain this relationship. We first started dating in early June of 2008 and the last time I saw Kay was late December 2011, so I tried for about three and a half years to make it work. I can honestly say that in this type of situation it will most likely not work, in my opinion. Kay did not seek counseling or medication for the most part of this time duration. Looking back on this relationship I can truly see how twisted and deluded it was. Even just reading through these emails again is taxing on my emotions and mental state. I will never have a relationship with Kay again. The borderline life is not a life for me. I do not wish to take care of another adult that is in the role of a partner but plays the role of a dependent. It is a taxing lifestyle that I do not wish on any other human being. I am very surprised that I did in fact survive my time with Kay. There were many times that she had threatened to kill me in my sleep, or said that she was going to trade sexual favors to a desperate man in return for him taking my life, and many other threats of this nature. I could've been thrown in prison for Kay's delusional thoughts and memories and luckily I was not. But I know that if I were to ever return to her I would surly end up dead or in prison. I tip my hat to anybody who is better at dealing with situations like this —J.C.

www.ingramcontent.com/pod-product-compliance
Lightning Source LLC
Chambersburg PA
CBHW070118290526
45789CB00005B/2052